MW01643796

To Do:
nap
draw
scavenge
tidy up
nap
1006
SUMMIT
AVENUE
SOCIETY
EST. 1982
USA 44
Herb
1006 Summit Avenue
St. Paul, MN
55105
My favorite!
I hope you like the book!
Herb

The Minnesota Governor's Residence, located at 1006 Summit Avenue in the heart of Saint Paul, is a magnificent twenty room English Tudor home. The first building permit was issued in 1910 and construction was completed in 1912. The land was purchased for $7,000 and was one of the last desirable lots available. Built at an estimated cost of $50,000, the Residence contains 14,706 square feet on one acre of land.

The home is an excellent example of Beaux Arts Revival, designed by Minneapolis architect William Channing Whitney for Saint Paul lumberman Horace Hills Irvine. The Irvine family occupied the home from its completion in 1912 until 1965. In 1965, the two youngest daughters, Clothilde Irvine Moles and Olivia Irvine Dodge, generously donated 1006 Summit Avenue to the State of Minnesota to be used as the Governor's Residence.

The Governor's Residence is on both the National Register of Historic Places and the Saint Paul Historic Sites Register.

The 1006 Summit Avenue Society is a non-profit fundraising organization dedicated to preserving the grace and beauty of the Minnesota Governor's Residence. All proceeds from the sale of this book are donated directly to the 1006 Summit Avenue Society to support ongoing efforts to sustain the iconic elegance of our state treasure as it welcomes dignitaries and visitors from around the world.

The Governor's Mouse and related materials are available for purchase at www.minnesotasbookstore.com

Printed at Ideal Printers Inc. in St. Paul, MN.

First Edition: 2010

ISBN-13: 978-0-615-41627-4

Cover and interior design by Kirsten Sevig.

Illustrations were created in pen and ink with watercolor.
Herb's drawing were created with a blue colored pencil.

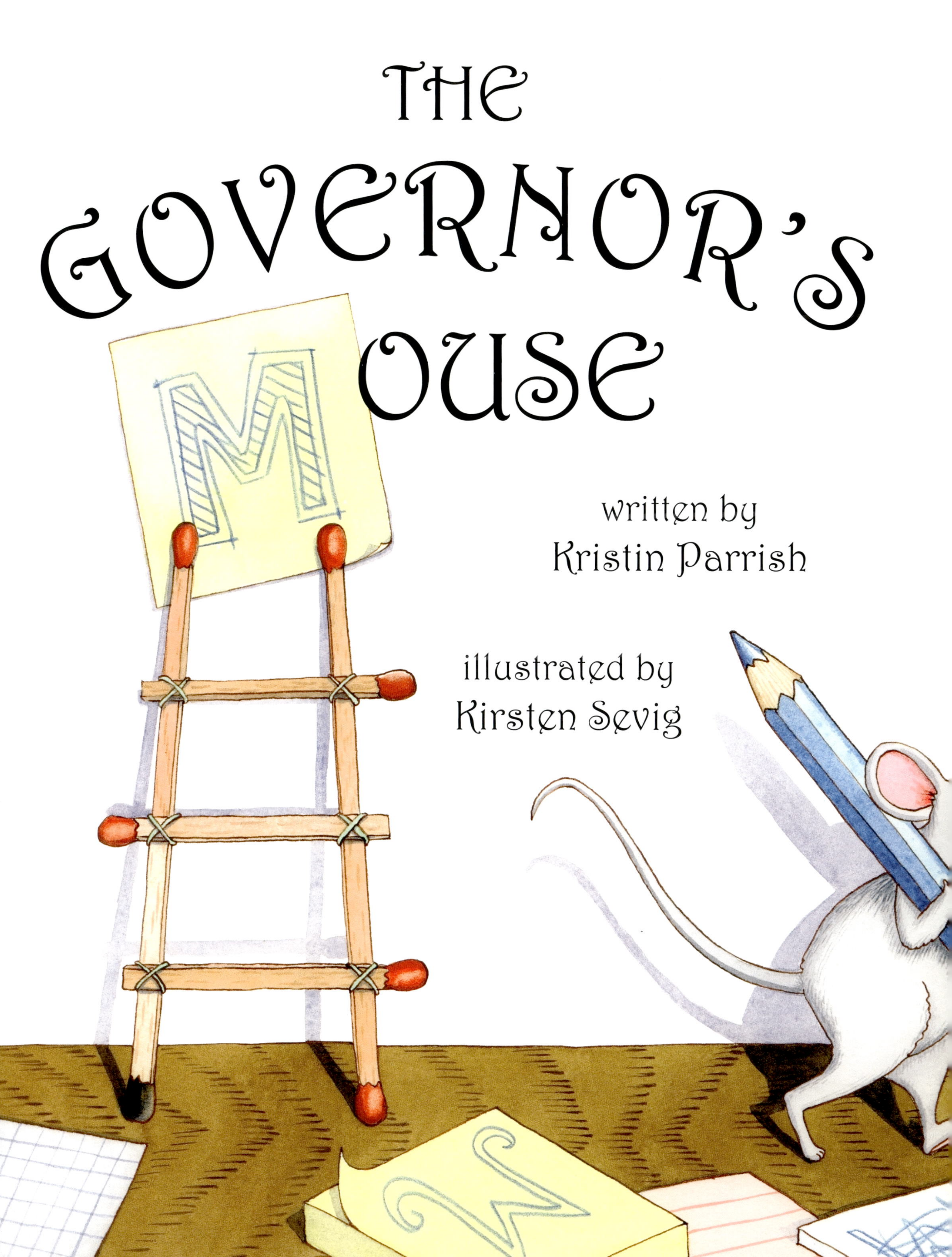
THE
GOVERNOR'S
MOUSE
written by
Kristin Parrish
illustrated by
Kirsten Sevig

Hello! I'm Herb and I'm a mouse.
I live in the Minnesota Governor's house
at Ten-O-Six Summit Avenue
and I'd like to show my home to you.

1006

There are beautiful gates where visitors stop
to admire the Residence from bottom to top.
I am so proud to watch them smile with pleasure
at this lovely and perfect Minnesota state treasure.

Please join me and walk to the grand front door...
I am glad you're here so I can tell you more.
In 1912, the Irvine family built this house.
If I'd been here then, I'd be a very old mouse!

After many years, they gave their home to the state.
It was an important decision
that was generous and great.
They donated their house for our Governors to live in.
It was a very big gift for someone to have given.

For every First Family, the plan is perfection
and the residents change with every election.
Except for me, I will always stay
at home in the Foyer, tucked out of the way.

There have been so many guests over the years to greet

but mostly I've tried to avoid their feet!

And here is my home, the best spot around
filled with treasures I have found.

HERB
POST

Here's a gallery of guests that have traveled through.
I wish I had time to sketch a portrait of you!
But we should continue the tour,
come on, let's scurry…
There are so many rooms! We need to hurry!

KEVIN GARNETT
MARIA SHRIVER
ELEANOR ROOSEVELT
MIKHAIL GORBACHEV
ROBIN WRIGHT

The Library is cozy and a good place to look
for a comfortable spot to read this very book.

The Solarium is a room
made mostly of glass
with windows for watching
the seasons pass.

The Dining Room is perfect for a mouse like me
to catch a snack during afternoon tea.

The Day Room is fancy with a piano that's grand.
I'd play you a tune, but I'd need a helping hand!

There is an attic up top and a basement below.
Some rooms are private and some are for show.

And if you can believe it, I swear that it's true!
There's a tunnel under the Residence, too!

But the garden is my favorite spot.
With the shade from the leaves,
it is never too hot.
I think I will rest here after we say goodbye...
This is a pretty big house for a little guy!

Thank you for coming. I wish you could stay.
Next time you visit, we'll have more time to play.
I hope you love this house as much as I do.
Come back soon. I'll be looking for you!